AMERICA IN WORLD WAR I

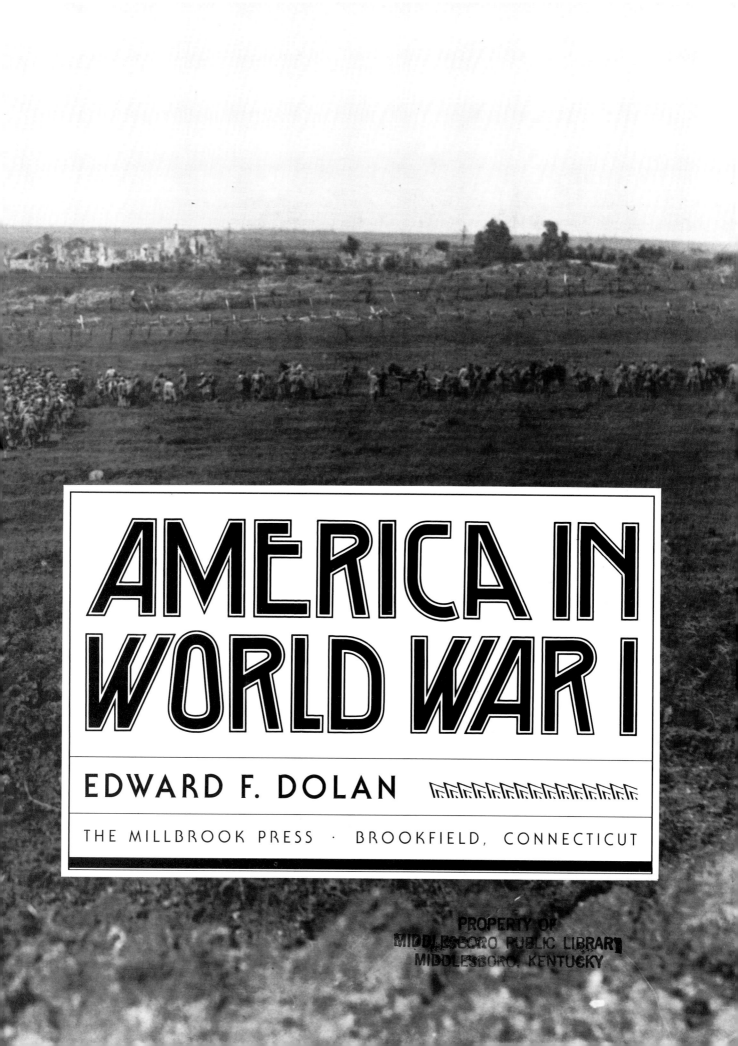

AMERICA IN WORLD WAR I

EDWARD F. DOLAN

THE MILLBROOK PRESS · BROOKFIELD, CONNECTICUT

Cover photograph courtesy of UPI/Bettmann

Photographs courtesy of the National Archives: pp. 2–3, 36, 37, 42, 51, 55, 60, 66, 71, 73, 74, 77, 78, 85; UPI/Bettmann: pp. 10, 13; Library of Congress: pp. 19, 20, 26, 29, 31, 34, 38, 47, 53, 58, 83, 85, 88; Imperial War Museum: pp. 44, 54; AP/Wide World: p. 62. Maps by Frank Senyk.

Published by The Millbrook Press, Inc.
2 Old New Milford Road, Brookfield, Connecticut 06804

Library of Congress Cataloging-in-Publication Data
Dolan, Edward F., 1924–
America in World War I / Edward F. Dolan.
p.   cm.
Includes bibliographical references and index.
Summary: Explains the roots of World War I and shows how the United States was drawn in despite strong sentiment for remaining uninvolved. Actions of U.S. troops "over there," new weapons such as the tank and airplane, the home front, and the peace that ended the war are covered.
ISBN 1-56294-522-X (lib. bdg.)
1. World War, 1914–1918—United States—Juvenile literature.
I. Title.
D522.7.D65   1996
940.3'73—dc20   95-35487   CIP   AC

CONTENTS

AMERICA IN WORLD WAR I

THE CALL TO WAR

PRESIDENT WOODROW WILSON'S face was grim as he stepped to the rostrum. He was in the House of Representatives to address a joint session of the United States Congress. He looked out at the sea of faces in the great chamber. They were all as grim as his. Everyone knew what he was going to say. He was about to ask the members of the House and Senate to declare war on Germany.

The date was April 2, 1917. For almost three years, the president had striven to keep the nation out of the war that was raging in Europe and in other areas around the world. But the actions of Germany during those years had finally made it impossible for America to remain neutral in the fighting.

The president began to speak in a quiet, sad voice. His listeners knew that he regretted every word. He hated war and, along with trying to preserve his country's neutrality, had tried—and failed—to get the warring nations to lay down their arms.

Woodrow Wilson, president of the United States from 1913 to 1921, had tried to keep the country out of war for as long as possible. By 1917, however, he asked Congress to declare war on Germany.

Now his listeners heard him describe those vain efforts. He went on to outline the German actions that had made it impossible for America to continue its neutral stance. The most hateful of those actions had been Germany's submarine attacks on merchant ships suspected of carrying war materials to Europe. Among the victims of these attacks had been a number of American freighters.

According to maritime law, a nation at war had the right to stop and search the merchant ships of a neutral country that were suspected of carrying war materials to the enemy. It also had the right to capture or destroy a merchant ship found to be carrying such goods. It did *not*, however, have the right to sink a neutral ship without prior warning and without first removing its crew to safety. The attacker could not leave them to fend for themselves in the sea. But this was exactly what Germany had done in recent weeks to four U.S. freighters, at a cost of more than a hundred American seamen.

Wilson now said that the United States was not going to make war on the German people. The country had only the deepest sympathy for them. Rather, the war would be waged against their "military masters," the warriors who had led them into a terrible conflict and had authorized the submarine attacks on U.S. shipping. The attacks, he said, left no doubt that Germany was already making war on America. Tonight he was asking Congress to issue a resolution to fight back.

He concluded with the ringing statement that right is more precious than peace and that:

> . . . we shall fight for the things which we have always carried nearest our hearts—for democracy . . . for the rights and liberties of small nations. . . . The day has come when America is privileged to spend her blood and her might for the principles that gave her birth, happiness and the peace which she has treasured. . . .

Tumultuous applause rocked the House chamber at the close of the speech. Still, the president was saddened by what he had done. But he knew that Germany had given him just one choice—to ask Congress for a declaration of war.

On April 4, the Senate responded to that request by declaring war on Germany. The House of Representatives did the same on Good Friday, April 6, 1917. America was now in a worldwide conflict that had erupted three years earlier, when a young man in the distant European city of Sarajevo had stepped off the sidewalk and fired a pistol at two people in a passing car.

DEATH IN SARAJEVO

The young, dark-haired man stood nervously at the street corner, one hand clutching a pistol in his coat pocket. His name was Gavrilo Princip, and he was standing at the corner for one reason. He hoped to assassinate Archduke Francis Ferdinand of Austria, the man who would soon replace the aged Francis Joseph on the throne of the Austrian-Hungarian empire.

June 28, 1914, was a bright Sunday in Sarajevo, the capital city of Princip's beloved country, Bosnia, a little nation that had been made a part of Austria six years before. Like many Bosnians, Princip wanted Bosnia to be free again. He was willing to do anything—including murder a future emperor—to help win that freedom.

Princip was not alone in his willingness to kill the archduke, who was visiting Sarajevo to review the Bosnian army. With him were six companions, who had all pledged to do away with Ferdinand. Five had lost their nerve and had done nothing. The sixth had taken action that morning as Ferdinand's open car passed in a procession of automobiles through the streets. He had hurled a hand grenade at the vehicle, but it missed its target and exploded beneath the next car in line, wounding several army officers and twenty spectators.

Princip was filled with anger and hope—anger at his ineffectual colleagues and hope that he himself now had

Archduke Francis Ferdinand of Austria and his wife, Sophie, whose assassinations in Sarajevo, Bosnia, led to the start of the Great War.

the chance to succeed where they had failed. He had learned that the grenade attack would not keep Ferdinand from riding through the streets that afternoon in another motorized parade. The archduke was now on his way to a hospital to visit one of the morning's victims. And so Princip stood at the street corner—waiting.

Suddenly, Princip heard the people along the sidewalk begin to shout. Ferdinand's open car came into view and moved toward him. He could see the chauffeur and three passengers: Ferdinand, his wife Sophie, and the governor of Bosnia. His hand tightened about the pistol. He hoped his targets would not speed past before he could take aim.

Then his mouth fell open. He could not believe his luck. The car was slowing as it approached. Miraculously, it stopped right in front of him, because the chauffeur was unsure whether to turn at the corner or drive straight ahead. Ferdinand in his splendid uniform and Sophie in her white dress sat no more than a few feet away from Princip.

Out came the pistol. Princip pushed through the crowd and dashed into the street. Two gunshots shattered the air. One bullet struck the archduke in the neck and threw him back against the seat cushions. The second missed its target—the governor—and struck Sophie. She fell to one side.

Princip had just time enough to see blood rushing from Archduke Ferdinand's mouth before he was surrounded by police and dragged away to be arrested. Only later did he learn that his two victims were dead and that, on this June day in 1914, he had hurled Europe along the road to the disaster that would soon be known as the Great War and, years later, as World War I.

THE ROAD TO DISASTER

THE AMERICAN PEOPLE watched in shock as the nations of Europe took sides and prepared for war in the wake of the killings in Sarajevo. Tragic though the assassinations were, many wondered how the deaths of two people could lead to fighting that would surely sacrifice countless more lives.

To find the answer, we must understand the history of the Slavic people of eastern Europe. In 1914 they were divided into two groups: the Austrian Slavs and the Serbian Slavs. The former, among them the Bosnians, lived within Austria. The latter occupied the small neighboring country of Serbia.

The Serbians wanted to wrest Bosnia from Austria and make it a part of their own country. Archduke Ferdinand was soon to replace his aged uncle, Francis Joseph, as the emperor of the Austrian-Hungarian empire.

The Serbians feared he would make changes in the Austrian government that would please the Bosnians and, although many Bosnians hated Austria, make them unwilling to break away and join Serbia.

To prevent this from happening, the Serbians launched a vicious propaganda campaign against Austria. In addition, a Serbian terrorist group—the Black Hand—plotted to kill Ferdinand and throw Austria into chaos. They recruited Princip and his six companions for the grisly task.

The angry Austrian government suspected, correctly, that the Serbians were behind the assassinations. It sent an ultimatum to Serbia, insisting that the little country agree to ten demands in order to avoid war with Austria. The most important were the final two: that Austrian officials be allowed to enter Serbia and quash the propaganda campaign; and that Austria take part in investigating the killings and punishing the participants.

Serbia had a giant friend—Russia. The Austrian government knew that if Serbia rejected its demands war with one would also mean war with the other. So, before delivering the ultimatum, Austria had turned to its longtime allies, the Germans, and asked if they would come to its aid in the event of war with Russia. The answer was yes.

Austria delivered the ultimatum to Serbia on July 23, 1914. Serbia answered that it would accept all the demands except the all-important final two. Calling the response "unsatisfactory," Austria declared war on Serbia on July 28.

The situation was bad, but it worsened as the major European powers took sides in the newborn conflict. Almost every day, there was more frightening news:

July 29: Russia began to mobilize to come to Serbia's defense.

July 31: The German government told Russia to stop the mobilization or risk war with Germany. The Russians were given twelve hours to reply to the demand. The German government also sent a message to France, asking if France would support Russia against Germany.

August 1: No reply to the July 31 message was received from the Russians. Germany declared war on Russia.

August 3: France had not replied to Germany's message, but had begun mobilizing. Germany was certain the French would side with the Russians and declared war on France.

Why, many Americans asked, were these nations taking sides? Fear was the answer. The European countries had long worried about what could happen if any one of them ever grew too powerful. They were afraid that the very powerful would seek to expand their territories by invading their neighbors' lands, or would attempt to enrich themselves by encroaching on those neighbors' foreign trade with overseas colonies. To protect themselves against these dangers, the nations formed mutual-defense pacts with their friends.

In 1879, Germany and Austria-Hungary had made a treaty in which they agreed to help each other in any war with Russia. The two countries were known as the Central Powers because they were located in central Europe. In 1894, France and Russia promised to fight together should either be attacked by Germany. Great Britain and France made the same agreement in 1904. Then, three years later, Britain joined Russia in a similar pact. Britain, France, and Russia became known as the Allied Powers.

Because of these treaties, the opponents in the war—the Central Powers on one side and the Allied Powers on the other—were established long before the assassinations in Sarajevo.

AUGUST 4, 1914

Though the nations rattled their swords in June and July, there was no actual fighting. Instead, several countries attempted to end the conflict peacefully before it began. All the efforts failed, however.

Great Britain played a leading role in those peacemaking efforts and, despite its mutual-defense pacts with France and Russia, had yet to declare war on Germany. The British leaders kept hoping that somehow peace could be preserved. Germany's emperor, Kaiser Wilhelm II, then set out to invade France, however, and changed their mind.

Every European military man knew that one of the easiest ways to enter France from Germany was to march down through Belgium to the French northern border. On August 4, Kaiser Wilhelm sent his troops crashing into Belgium. The Belgian army, determined to defend its land, met the invaders head on. Suddenly, the quiet conflict turned into a shooting war.

Just as suddenly, the British declared war on Germany. As had other European nations, Britain had long ago pledged to defend Belgium's neutrality in any war. It now kept its word.

Americans everywhere read the news reports of the first fighting. Then, in the next months, they learned that other European countries were entering the fray. Turkey joined Germany at the end of 1914, and Bulgaria

Kaiser Wilhelm II, emperor of Germany. Austria-Hungary and Germany were allies in the war, and were known as the Central Powers.

followed suit in 1915. In that same year, Italy chose to fight with the Allied Powers.

Far across the world, in August 1914, Japan entered the fighting against Germany because of its dislike of Germany's colonial presence in the Orient. China took the same step in 1915.

When all was said and done, the opposing sides were aligned as follows:

In August 1914, Germany invaded France by crossing Belgium, which forced Belgium and its ally Great Britain to enter the war. In this photo, Germans are marching through Place Charles Rogier in Brussels.

THE ALLIED POWERS

Great Britain (and its empire holdings, including Canada and Australia)
France
Russia
Belgium
Italy
Montenegro (a neighbor of Bosnia)
Serbia
Japan
China
Portugal
Romania
Greece

THE CENTRAL POWERS

Germany
Austria-Hungary
Bulgaria
Turkey

Now only one major nation was not in the war—the United States. That would change in 1917, but in the meantime the conflict turned America into a country at war with itself. Its people were first sharply divided over which side to support and then over whether or not it should join in the fighting.

MOVING TOWARD WAR

AS SOON AS the fighting erupted, President Woodrow Wilson declared the United States' neutrality in the war. Neutrality meant that, in addition to not going into battle, the nation would remain friendly with the warring sides. Each would be treated the same way.

Because he greatly admired England and its culture, Wilson personally favored the Allied cause. The president, however, kept his feelings to himself. But the American people did not. They quickly spoke out and showed how sharply divided they were over which side to support.

Some refused to take sides at all. Arguing that the Europeans were always fighting, they said they wanted no part of this new fight. A great many more favored the Allies because of a preference for Britain and France.

Of the 100 million people in the United States, the 50 million who traced their roots back to Britain and Canada had sympathy for the British. Support for the French was due to the help that France had given the American colonies in the Revolutionary War. There was a widespread feeling that the United States owed France a debt that could never be fully repaid.

The Central Powers also had their supporters: some 12 million Americans whose forebears had come from Germany, Austria-Hungary, Bulgaria, and Turkey. Joining them were Americans of Irish descent, whose longtime enemy was Britain, which had held their ancient homeland under its thumb for nine centuries.

WATCHING THE WAR

From August to October 1914, Americans devoured news reports of Germany's entry into Belgium. As the invaders moved toward France and knocked the Belgian troops out of the way, they spread out along a front that extended from west to east across the width of the little country. French, British, and Indian troops swept in and put a stop to the enemy advance near the city of Ypres at the western end of the front, just short of the French border.

To the east, however, the Germans moved into France and toward Paris. They were finally halted in vicious fighting along the Marne River, which lay to the northeast of the French capital.

At the same time, there was fighting on France's eastern border. French troops burst into Alsace-Lorraine, a region that France had lost to Germany in the Franco-Prussian War of 1870 and had been determined to regain ever since. They were thrown back by a superior German force.

By October, the fighting had cost both sides dearly. In mere weeks, each had lost more than a half million men, who were killed, wounded, or captured. Neither had won a clear-cut victory, and the fighting had reached a stalemate.

Exhausted, the opponents dug a network of defensive trenches along what became known as the western front—an area of almost 500 miles (805 kilometers) that ran through Belgium, across northern France, and then south along the French-German border to Switzerland. The people of Europe had hoped that the war would not be a long one, but the digging marked the start of years of trench warfare—tragic years during which soldiers lived in filth and launched unsuccessful offensives through enemy lines heavily defended with machine guns and barbed wire.

Those same years—1914 to 1918—brought word of fighting elsewhere. German and Russian troops battled along the eastern front, a vast area stretching along and beyond Germany's eastern border. In the Pacific Ocean, Japanese forces captured a series of German possessions, among them the Caroline, Mariana, and Marshall islands. The British attacked Turkey and Germany's African holdings: Togo, Cameroon, German Southwest Africa, and German Southeast Africa.

A PROFITABLE WAR

Though horrible to watch, the war was a financial boon for America. The nation had been in the grip of a severe economic depression for months, and now it happily saw the bad times suddenly end as both the Allied and Central Powers began ordering food and war materials from the United States. Farms and factories began to hum with activity again, and thousands of jobless people went back to work.

From 1914 until America's entry into the war in 1917, the nation sent more than $3 billion in needed goods—arms, vehicles, clothing, and food—to Britain. Over $1 billion in goods went to France and more than $383 million to Germany.

A SHIFT OF SYMPATHY

While there continued to be some public support for both sides, most U.S. sympathy went to the Allies as the war progressed. This shift took place for several reasons. First, the German invasion had ripped Belgium to pieces. Cities were destroyed, the countryside was reduced to a muddy ruin, and the people were left starving. Americans donated money, food, and clothing to help relieve the suffering nation.

Next, there were the tales that Allied diplomats in the United States told about the German invaders. They depicted the green-uniformed soldiers as "barbarian Huns" who killed civilians, raped women, and bayoneted infants as they crashed through Belgium. Although there are always brutalities on both sides in a war, these stories were propaganda and had little or no truth to them. Much of the American public accepted these tales as factual, however, and the German soldier was soon widely seen as a cruel beast.

The most important reason of all for the shift of sympathy was Germany's use of a new weapon of war—the submarine, or, as it was known to the Germans, the U-boat (from the word *Unterseebooten*, "underwater boat").

The German *Unterseebooten,* or U-boat, showed for the first time the power of the submarine as a weapon of war. From 1914 to 1918, German U-boats sank more than 11 million tons of Allied shipping and killed thousands of men.

Though it had been tried in America's Revolutionary and Civil Wars, the submarine showed its true effectiveness for the first time in a German blockade of the waters off Ireland and England.

SUBMARINE WARFARE

The story of the U-boat begins at the very start of the war. Britain had thrown up a sea blockade off Germany's western coast to keep enemy and neutral merchant ships from reaching Germany with war supplies.

Immediately, British warships had begun to capture enemy freighters. Merchant ships from neutral countries, including the United States, were stopped and searched as they approached the blockade. If they were carrying enemy supplies, they were turned away.

The blockade was choking off all supplies to Germany, and so the Germans responded with a blockade of their own. Their blockade was unlike its British counterpart, however. It was not created by warships but by the many U-boats Germany had built. The small submarines would prowl the waters around Britain and Ireland and sink any enemy ship that lumbered into sight. The Germans said that they would try to avoid sinking neutral vessels, but warned that there might be "unfortunate accidents." They also warned the people of neutral countries not to travel on ships owned by the enemy.

Both of these warnings angered President Wilson. He saw them as threats to America's right to the freedom of the seas. He told the Germans that they would be held strictly accountable for any attacks on U.S. lives or shipping.

The U-boats proved to be deadly weapons. Between 1914 and 1918, they sank more than 11 million tons of Allied shipping and killed thousands of merchant sailors and others. The U-boats were the German weapon that eventually drew America into the war.

The trouble began in 1915. In May, a U-boat torpedoed the American oil tanker *Gulflight* and sent the ship to the bottom of the sea. German leaders called the sinking one of those "unfortunate accidents" they had warned of and offered to pay the United States for the loss of the vessel. Six days later, a U-boat torpedo smashed into the British passenger liner *Lusitania* as it approached Ireland. The ship sank within an hour and took 1,198 people to their deaths. Among the dead were 128 Americans, some of them women and children. Finally, in August, German torpedoes struck the British liner *Arabic* and cost two more Americans their lives.

The deaths of innocent passengers aboard the *Lusitania* and *Arabic* outraged the American public. Though both ships were victims of war activities, they were protected by maritime law in the same way that merchant ships were. According to these laws, the ships could not be sunk without prior warning and without first putting their crews and passengers safely ashore. The subs had not observed these rules and had attacked by surprise. In American eyes, the U-boat captains and crewmen were murderers.

In German eyes, however, the maritime law was impossible for the subs to obey and the surprise attacks had been necessary. The subs were small and lightly armed. To give advance warning of attack, they had to surface. They dared not do this for fear of being rammed by their prey or bombarded by guns concealed aboard the intended target. Nor did they have the space to take on the victim's passengers and crew for the trip to shore. The Germans felt, therefore, that the subs were forced to strike by surprise.

The sinkings of these ships brought angry protests from the U.S. government. The protests were successful. Following the *Arabic* tragedy, the Germans promised not to sink passenger liners without prior warning. The promise somewhat cooled American tempers, which had become so hot that many people were demanding that the United States declare war on Germany. Others, who wanted no part of a European conflict or of any

war, vehemently opposed this demand. The nation was now more divided than it ever had been over the question of which side to support.

The cooling period lasted until March 1916. Then, a German U-boat attacked the *Sussex,* a small British liner that was being used by the French. The ship sank in the English Channel, with the loss of eighty civilians, among them several Americans. The call for war—as well as the opposition to it—grew.

Outraged, President Wilson told the German government that it must now stop the surprise attacks on passenger and merchant vessels. If they refused, the United

THE ZIMMERMANN NOTE

In early 1917, Arthur Zimmermann, the German foreign minister, sent a note to the president of Mexico. In it he proposed a German-Mexican alliance if the United States declared war on Germany. As repayment, Zimmermann promised to return the states of Texas, New Mexico, and Arizona to Mexico should the United States be defeated. These states included lands that Mexico had lost to America in the Mexican War of 1847.

Zimmermann also urged the Mexican president to convince Japan to abandon the Allied side and join the Central Powers, all in return for whatever spoils the country could claim from the United States in the event of an Allied defeat.

The message was intercepted by British intelligence agents, turned over to the United States government, and then made public by officials in Washington, D.C. The disclosure of this note added to the fury that many Americans felt against Germany because of the U-boat attacks and intensified their demand that America join in the war.

The death of American citizens aboard passenger and merchant vessels enraged the American people, and eventually led to the United States' declaration of war against Germany.

States would sever its diplomatic ties with Germany. Such a step would almost certainly lead to war. Wilson's action prompted a new pledge from Germany: Its U-boats would no longer attack *any* neutral ships without warning.

Again, U.S. tempers cooled, but the new pledge could not be kept. The British blockade was strangling Germany. Desperately needed food and supplies were not reaching their destinations, and the German people were beginning to starve. Yet the country's U-boats were forced to stand by helplessly as supply-laden neutral freighters sailed into Britain. Consequently, in January 1917, the German government announced that it was unleashing its undersea killers again. They would now sink *all* merchant ships—even those flying U.S. colors—that dared to come near.

In addition, the Germans knew that Britain, despite the flow of supplies it was receiving, was suffering greatly after the nearly four years of war. The Germans felt that its U-boat attacks might now knock the British out of the war.

Wilson responded by breaking off diplomatic relations with Germany in early February. He did not declare war on the country—at least not just yet. He did not believe that the German U-boats would actually attack American vessels. He said that any decision to make war would have to wait until there were "overt" acts by Germany against U.S. lives and property.

The wait was not long. In mid-March, U-boats sank four American freighters and took the lives of thirty-six U.S. seamen.

This was too much. The president called for a joint session of Congress and stepped before the legislators on April 2, his face grim.

America was going to war.

INTO BATTLE

LONG BEFORE APRIL 2, 1917, many Americans could see that the country was headed for war. They knew that the United States was ill prepared for the fighting.

The navy was strong, yes, but not the army. In 1915, it consisted of about 100,000 regular soldiers and had no more than a two-day supply of shells for its artillery. The artillery itself was sadly out of date.

Earlier that year, a number of prominent figures had begun to urge the nation to prepare for the war that was sure to come. Among them was former President Theodore Roosevelt. He led the way in establishing a string of summer camps for the officers who would soon be needed. The country was so short of arms that the future officers had to train with broomsticks instead of rifles.

By 1916, President Wilson himself had to admit that the chances that America would enter the war were steadily mounting. Although still hoping for peace, Wilson asked Congress to strengthen the nation's military. The legislators responded by passing the National Defense Act, which called for the army to expand to 175,000 men and the National Guard (made up of troops from each of the states) to 450,000 men. In addition to the National Defense Act, there were two congressional grants for ship construction—$313 million for warships and $50 million for merchant vessels.

These government measures increased the divisiveness that the prospect of war was causing among the American people. As soon as war was declared, however, a wave of patriotism washed over the country, and thousands of young men rushed to join the army, navy, and the marine corps. Young women everywhere enlisted as

I WANT YOU FOR U.S. ARMY
NEAREST RECRUITING STATION

Recruitment posters such as this one by artist James Montgomery Flagg inspired patriotic men and women throughout the country to enlist for military service.

nurses or replaced the men in offices and factories and on the nation's farms.

The final step toward preparedness was taken in May 1917, when Congress passed the Selective Service Act. It authorized the president to increase the size of the army and to bring the National Guard into federal service. Of particular importance, it gave Wilson the power to increase the army's strength through the use of a draft, a system for selecting individuals for military service.

In early June 1917, some 9.5 million men between ages twenty-one and thirty registered for the draft and received identification numbers. Then, at mid-month, the numbers of more than 1.3 million men were drawn in a lottery. The first draftees went off to training camp, and thousands more soon followed them. Eventually, the draft would include men aged eighteen to forty-five.

The new soldiers received an average of six months of training. While the first of them were traveling to hastily built tent camps, the army was preparing to send regular troops to France. Before those troops could safely cross the Atlantic, however, a path had to be cut for them through the U-boat-infested waters off Ireland and the southern coast of England.

The job of clearing that path fell to the U.S. Navy and, in particular, to the officer who was selected to command the country's naval forces in Europe: Rear Admiral William Sowden Sims.

A PATH THROUGH THE SEA

Soon after America declared war, Sims arrived in England and met with Britain's chief naval officer, Admiral

The Selective Service Act allowed the president to increase the army through the draft system. More than a million draftees left for training camps in early June 1917.

Sir John Jellicoe. Jellicoe told Sims how much harm the German subs were doing. In April alone, they had sunk 900,000 tons of British-bound shipping, sometimes more than nine ships a week. Britain was running dangerously low on supplies. Unless more merchant ships began reaching port, the nation might soon be forced out of the war. Some way had to be found to reduce or end the losses.

Sims had a suggestion—one that could reduce the losses and, at the same time, make the Atlantic crossing safer for U.S. troops. Until now, the merchant ships had traveled alone and had been easy prey. Sims advised that they travel in convoys protected by fast-moving naval escorts—destroyers and cruisers. The escorts might scare off the U-boats or strike back with guns and depth charges if the subs attacked.

Sims's idea was not a new one. The British had already considered and rejected it. They disliked the thought of dozens of ships traveling close together. There was danger of collision if the vessels were forced to travel without lights, especially in heavy fog and at night. Further, Britain did not have enough cruisers and destroyers to contribute to the convoys—they were needed elsewhere in the worldwide conflict.

Troops scaling walls at Camp Wadsworth in South Carolina as part of their basic training.

AT WAR ON THE HOME FRONT

No matter how divided they had been, once the United States entered the war, people at home quickly got to work providing the materials needed for the fighting. Crowding into factories all across the country, they began to produce everything from munitions to uniforms. Before the war ended, they had turned out, among other equipment, a half-million rifles, 3.5 billion bullets, and 20 million artillery shells.

FOOD WILL WIN THE WAR

You came here seeking Freedom
You must now help to preserve it

WHEAT is needed for the allies
Waste nothing

UNITED STATES FOOD ADMINISTRATION

One of the most important home-front tasks was to grow food, not only for the soldiers overseas and stateside but also for America's families and the people of the beleaguered Allied nations. Thousands of men and women went to work on farms, increasing the nation's agricultural output by 25 percent. To make sure that the growing food supply was not wasted, the government urged the conservation of food. Everyone was asked to save leftovers for future meals. "Meatless Tuesdays" and "Porkless Thursdays" were introduced. Children were reminded to be "patriotic to the core" when eating apples and to waste nothing.

Another major task for those left at home was the construction of the ships needed to carry soldiers, equipment, and foodstuffs overseas. The government launched a huge shipbuilding program that eventually employed 350,000 workers in 341 shipyards. These workers produced hundreds of merchant vessels at a blinding rate of speed. On July 4, 1918, alone, ninety-five new ships were launched.

By 1918 the war was costing $44 million a day. To raise the needed money, the government increased taxes and embarked on a program of Liberty Loans. Under the loan program, Americans could purchase government bonds for a few dollars or, when children bought them, a few cents. The government promised to repay the loans at a later date and to add a profit in the form of interest. Liberty Loan campaigns brought in a total of more than $21 billion in sales.

Unfortunately, despite all the fine work and spirit going into the war effort, there was an ugly side to life on the home front. The nation's German Americans became the victims of a hate-inspired hysteria that gripped the United States immediately before the war and that lasted throughout it. This hysteria led to a variety of injustices. The teaching of the German language was banned in many high schools and universities. Eggs and garbage were thrown at some German American homes. Worst of all, a number (thankfully small) of innocent Germans were physically beaten, and one man was lynched by a drunken mob.

Some German Americans changed their names for safety's sake. Also changed were the names of things that had their origins in the German language. Hamburger steak and the German measles were rechristened "Liberty steak" and "Liberty measles." The dachshund dog was given the new name "Liberty pup."

Congress passed the Espionage Act of 1917 and the Sedition Act of 1918, both aimed against possible spying and sabotage activities. Both were triggered in part by the anger of the times and in part by the valid worry that some German Americans (and others opposed to the war) might attempt to harm or slow the nation's home-front effort. About 1,900 cases were tried under the acts, although most of them came to nothing.

The hysteria was a waste of time and energy. The vast majority of German Americans were loyal citizens, and thousands of young German American men joined the armed forces and fought overseas.

In response to this last argument, Sims promised that the United States would contribute the needed escort vessels. Heartened by his pledge, the British agreed to give the convoy system a try. In May the admiral began sending American destroyers into the danger zone. Three months later, there were forty-seven U.S. warships in convoy service. Among these warships was the destroyer *Fanning*, which was to win a special place in the history of World War I.

On a windswept November day in 1917, while helping to shepherd a convoy through the waters off Ireland, the *Fanning*'s crew sighted a periscope amidst the distant waves. The periscope vanished in seconds, but the destroyer swept to the spot where it had been seen and loosed a pattern of depth charges there. Other escort ships joined the attack.

For a time, it seemed as if the depth charges had failed to do their job. No oil or debris, telltale signs of a destroyed sub, floated to the surface. The *Fanning*'s sailors grumbled in disappointment, certain that the U-boat had escaped. Then, suddenly, the water near them erupted, and the submarine burst into view. Its crew rushed out on deck, their arms raised in surrender.

The *Fanning* closed in and hauled the Germans aboard. Then the Americans learned what had happened aboard the sub. The depth charges had not damaged the hull, but had destroyed the navigation gear. The sub's commander, rather than struggle blindly beneath the waves and risk death for his crew, had come to the surface. This was the first German U-boat to be captured by the American Navy.

The convoy system was a magnificent success. By the close of 1917, the monthly loss of ships to U-boat attacks was reduced to 400,000 tons, 500,000 tons less than the toll had been in April. The convoys had also cleared a path for the safe arrival of the Americans. By the dawn of 1918, some 50,000 troops a month were landing in Europe. The number of monthly landings rose to 100,000 in the spring and then to 300,000 by mid-1918. Troops traveled across the Atlantic on U.S. transports, British liners, and German ships that had been in stateside ports when war was declared and had been commandeered by the U.S. Army. Of all those who went overseas, only 100 died en route. They drowned when an enemy torpedo slammed into the transport *Ticonderoga*.

PERSHING AND THE AMERICAN EXPEDITIONARY FORCE

The U.S. troops who sailed overseas were known as the American Expeditionary Force (AEF). Assigned to command them was fifty-seven-year-old John J. "Black Jack" Pershing, a silver-haired, ramrod-straight officer who had served in the army since graduating from West Point in 1886. He was a man of firm opinions, and two of these opinions were going to help America play a vital role in ending the war.

First, Pershing was opposed to the plans that the French and British had for his troops. Both nations doubted that the AEF, which was chiefly made up of raw recruits, would be a valuable fighting force on its own. They wanted to assign the newcomers to French and British units as replacements for the men that the war had claimed. Pershing knew that with this plan his soldiers would be sacrificed as "cannon fodder" for the

The convoy system, suggested by U.S. Rear Admiral William Sowden Sims, was an effective way to protect ships that were crossing the Atlantic, ensuring the safe arrival of British supplies and American troops. Destroyers and cruisers traveled alongside the merchant ships and transports and could strike back when German submarines attacked.

two countries, and he turned it down flat. He insisted that the AEF act as an independent force, as a partner in the war rather than a manpower pool for France and Britain.

Second, he loathed the idea of trench warfare. On his tours of the 500-mile-long (805-kilometer) western front, he saw the vile conditions that the soldiers daily endured. Their lives were spent huddled in mud and in damp, foul-smelling dugouts. Their constant companions were rats, lice, and infection.

Even worse from a military standpoint, he knew that trench warfare would never lead to victory but only to more killing. He had only to look back over the past

1915

The year brought Allied offensives in both Belgium and northern France. They had gained little ground but had exacted a terrible cost in life. The French had suffered 200,000 casualties; the British, 100,000; and the Germans 140,000.

(Throughout this book, British casualties will include those of Britain's empire holdings, among them Canada, Australia, India, and South Africa.)

1916

In February, a massive German force struck at the French trenches near the city of Verdun in northeastern France. At first, the Germans won a few miles, but then were pushed back almost to their starting point. The cost: 542,000 casualties for the French and 434,000 for the Germans.

two and a half years to see the truth of this. The Allies and the Germans had launched major offensives and suffered thousands of casualties (men killed, wounded, or missing in action), while trying to break through the enemy's heavily defended trenches.

In 1917, Pershing could only shake his head at the terrible loss of Allied and German life. He knew the two sides would go on needlessly sacrificing men for as long as the trench warfare continued.

Victory, Pershing insisted, could be won in only one way. The Allies had to mount a giant offensive that would drive the Germans from their trenches and push them back into open country. Once the Germans were in the open, the Allies could sweep through Germany and bring the enemy to its knees. To make certain that the AEF would be prepared for that offensive, the general ordered the training camps at home to coach the soldiers in mobile, "open country" warfare. That training was to pay dividends in 1918.

Allied and German soldiers positioned in the hundreds of miles of trenches along the western front struggled with their muddy, pest-ridden living conditions as well as with the enemy.

FIRST TASTE OF BATTLE

The 1st Division, manned by 27,000 regular army soldiers, was the first U.S. unit sent to France. It arrived in June 1917, and was assigned to a sector of trenches near the Swiss border. This quiet sector was where the tired French and German soldiers, eager to avoid injury, had long engaged in a "pretend" war. Late each afternoon, they lobbed artillery shells at each other, always making sure that the shells landed harmlessly in "No Man's Land," the area separating the trenches.

Things changed when the Americans arrived. In October, not knowing about the "pretend" war, they opened the first U.S. artillery barrage of the war and fired their shells directly into a crowded German trench. Infuriated, the Germans retaliated a few days later. They bombarded the Americans and then sent 250 elite troops plunging across No Man's Land and into the U.S. trenches.

The attackers expected the Americans, untried as yet in battle, to flee in confusion. But the newcomers stood their ground in hand-to-hand fighting that lasted for just a few minutes before the Germans retreated, taking eleven prisoners with them. Left behind were the first U.S. soldiers to die in the war's trench fighting: Private Thomas Enright of Pennsylvania, Private Merle D. Hay of Iowa, and Corporal James B. Gresham of Indiana.

The 1st Division remained in the trenches throughout the rest of 1917. Far behind them, fresh AEF units poured into France. And, all the while, a new kind of warfare raged high above their heads.

AMERICAN WOMEN GO TO WAR

America's women were at work everywhere during World War I. They labored on the home front and overseas. They took jobs on the nation's farms, in factories, and in shipyards, and served in its military forces.

Approximately a million women filled the vacancies left by the men who were now in uniform. Many were young girls who had previously worked in local shops and department stores or who had never worked before. Many were wives who had once worked, but had left their jobs to raise families.

Women on the farms were nicknamed "farmerettes" by the press. In the factories and shipyards, they served mainly as clerks, secretaries, typists, and bookkeepers.

World War I also marked an important "first" for American women. For the first time in the nation's history, women were permitted to join the armed forces. Some 13,000, known as "Yeomanettes," enlisted in the navy to do clerical work stateside. Nearly 300 entered the marine corps as clerks and won the name "Marinettes." More than 230 women traveled to France as part of the U.S. Army Signal Corps. There, they served as telephone operators for the American Expeditionary Force (AEF).

But they were not the only ones to travel overseas. Some 11,000 women, although not actual members of the armed forces, served abroad (as well as at home) as nurses; others became ambulance drivers. Women were also among the 6,000 Red Cross workers who sailed to France.

About 3,500 women served in the cafeterias and recreation facilities that the Young Men's Christian Association (YMCA) operated in England, France, and Russia. Members of the Young Women's Christian Association (YWCA) also provided services for women overseas and at home. More than fifty women of the Society of Friends (the Quakers) tended wounded soldiers on the western front and helped to feed and clothe civilians who lost their homes in the fighting.

Two groups of American women also served on the western front before the United States entered the war. One group was

American women at work in the American Car & Foundry Company, Detroit, Michigan, camouflaging artillery vehicles.

made up of the wives and daughters of American diplomats who were stationed in Europe at the time the fighting erupted in 1914. They tended to the needs of families left homeless by the fighting. The other was a unit of ambulance drivers—the American Ambulance in Paris—formed by women living in France.

Like the men of the AEF, the 25,000 American women who served overseas risked death, disease, and injury. An estimated 348 lost their lives. Some were killed in air raids and artillery bombardments. Others died or were left debilitated by the diseases and disorders bred by the filthy and worse-than-primitive conditions along the western front.

The exact number of women who were injured is unknown. There are individual stories, however, that leave no doubt as to the seriousness of some of the injuries. When a hand grenade accidentally exploded near her, a writer and Red Cross worker sustained wounds that kept her hospitalized for two years. A woman doctor caught in a gas attack suffered burned lungs. A study conducted in the 1920s revealed that, among the women injured in the war, at least 200 were permanently disabled.

THE WAR IN THE AIR

THE MILITARY AIRPLANE was such a new weapon at the start of World War I that both sides were uncertain how to use it in the fighting. It soon proved useful in three ways: as a reconnaissance ship, a bomber, and a fighter.

ON RECONNAISSANCE DUTY

In 1914 the military plane was a fragile biplane with two open cockpits and a cloth skin, but it offered both sides a distinct advantage. It could travel over and above enemy lines. With its two-man crew—a pilot and an observer sitting behind him—this newcomer to war clattered over enemy territory to sight troop movements, sites of ammunition dumps, and gun emplacements. On returning home, the crew reported what they had seen so that the ground forces could better direct their artillery fire or know when an enemy attack seemed imminent.

When the fighting was just days old, the planes took off on the first of endless reconnaissance missions that they would fly in the war.

ON BOMBING DUTY

The airplane first went to work as a bomber because of what reconnaissance crews on both sides saw as they flew above Europe in August and September of 1914.

The crews of these aircraft knew that the soldiers and vehicles moving below them were vital targets and quickly armed themselves with whatever weapons were at hand. Sweeping low, they strafed the enemy troops with rifle and pistol fire or pelted them with hand grenades.

Within a few weeks, mechanics were fastening bomb racks to the undersides of the planes. At first, the racks were fitted with artillery shells that had been converted to bombs; later, they were fitted with bombs designed for air attacks.

The early bombing raids were haphazard affairs. The pilot sighted his prey, flew low over it, and released his payload at what he hoped was the right moment. Sometimes, he made a direct hit. More often, he was wide of the mark and was happy if he came anywhere near his target.

British fliers dropped down to only 500 feet (152 meters) before loosing their bombs. The idea was to hit within 50 feet (15 meters) of the target.

Haphazard though the attacks were, they were valuable to both sides. By 1915 both were working hard on their bombing skills. Both were also building heavier aircraft to handle the bomb weights. The earlier planes had been so lightweight that they could hardly get a load of several hundred pounds into the air. And both sides came up with bombsights to improve the accuracy of their attacks.

These advances led to the birth of strategic bombing. The planes no longer went after whatever prey they could find. Rather, they were assigned specific targets. Some targets were as far behind the front lines as the aircraft could fly without the risk of running out of fuel on the return home. The targets were all military (the bombings of civilian populations began in future wars) and ranged from war factories and shipyards to airfields and troop encampments.

Though effective, the airplane was not the *most* feared bomber early in the fighting. That distinction belonged to the German dirigible. Its range—close to 700 miles (1,126 kilometers) for the first models—enabled it to strike targets far beyond the reach of the plane. Germany produced 140 dirigibles during the war, all more than 500 feet (152 meters) in length.

Paris staggered under dirigible attacks thirty times between 1915 and war's end. London and several industrial areas in the center of England were hit fifty-four times during the same period. The dirigibles dropped 5,806 bombs on England, taking 557 lives and injuring 1,358 people.

In time, airplanes joined in these long-distance raids. Both the Allies and Germans developed bombing planes that had ranges of several hundred miles. The British and French launched 675 bombing raids against Germany between 1915 and the end of the war and dropped 543 tons of bombs. The planes built in Germany struck England fifty-two times, dropping 2,772 bombs that killed and injured almost 3,000 people.

German dirigibles—more than 500 feet (152 meters) long—were used as observation balloons and were the earliest effective bombers of the war. The Germans produced more than one hundred of these weapons during the war.

ON FIGHTER DUTY

The first reconnaissance planes on both sides carried no armament. After planes were hit by rifle fire from below, however, their crews equipped them with machine guns, which were usually mounted on the observer's cockpit, so that they could fight back. Soon, armed single-seat planes appeared. Their job was to down the enemy's reconnaissance planes and protect their own from attack. The result of this development was the emergence of the war's most famous planes—the fighters.

Despite the work done by the reconnaissance plane and the bomber, the fighter won the greatest fame in the war. Air battles—called dogfights—captured the imagination of the world. Fighter pilots, engaging in one-on-one combat far above the earth, were everywhere seen as modern versions of the heroic knights of old.

The first fighters were armed with machine guns mounted on the wings so that their bullets would not shatter the propeller, but the wingtop guns were difficult to aim. The planes needed guns placed just ahead of the pilot that could be fired without tearing the propeller to pieces. Both sides solved the problem with systems that sent the bullets flying between the spinning blades.

The most famous fighters were of French, British, and German design. The Spad VII ranked tops among French planes and was used by almost all the Allied forces. The Sopwith Camel was Britain's leading fighter. This plane, called the "Camel" because of the hump-shaped housing in which its guns were mounted, brought down more than 1,290 enemy planes. Germany's great fighter was the Fokker DrI; though clumsy looking because of its three wings, it proved to be highly maneuverable.

PUBLIC WARNING

The public are advised to familiarise themselves with the appearance of British and German Airships and Aeroplanes, so that they may not be alarmed by British aircraft, and may take shelter if German aircraft appear. **Should hostile aircraft be seen,** take shelter **immediately** in the nearest available house, preferably in the basement, and remain there until the aircraft have left the vicinity: do not stand about in crowds **and do not touch unexploded bombs.**

In the event of **HOSTILE** aircraft being seen in country districts, the nearest Naval, Military or Police Authorities should, if possible, be advised immediately by Telephone of the TIME OF APPEARANCE, the DIRECTION OF FLIGHT, **and whether the aircraft is an Airship or an Aeroplane.**

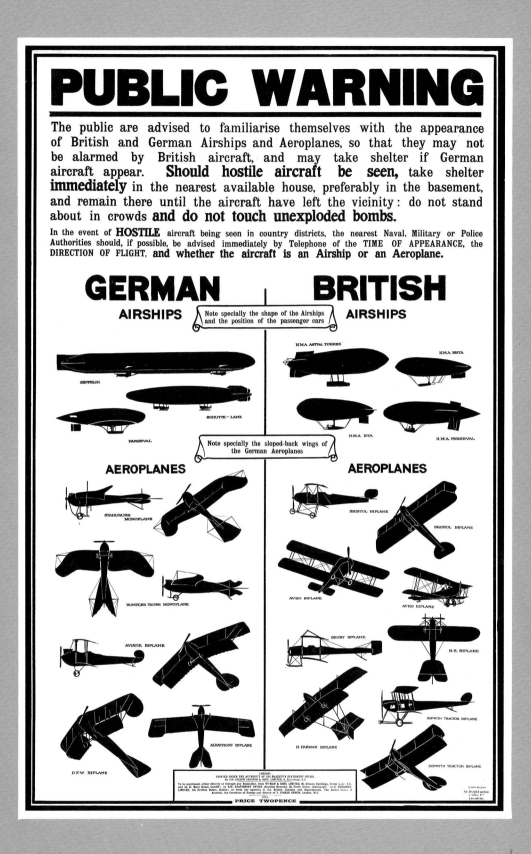

LONDON:
PRINTED UNDER THE AUTHORITY OF HIS MAJESTY'S STATIONERY OFFICE.
By SIR JOSEPH CAUSTON & SONS, LIMITED, 9, Eastcheap, E.C.
To be purchased, either directly or through any Bookseller, from WYMAN & SONS, LIMITED, 29, Breams Buildings, Fetter Lane, E.C.
and 54, St. Mary Street, Cardiff; or H.M. STATIONERY OFFICE (Scottish Branch), 23, Forth Street, Edinburgh; or E. PONSONBY,
LIMITED, 116, Grafton Street, Dublin; or from the Agencies in the British Colonies and Dependencies. The United States of
America, the Continent of Europe and Abroad of T. FISHER UNWIN, London, W.C.
1915.
PRICE TWOPENCE

COPYRIGHT
Sir Joseph Causton
& Sons, Ltd.
London.

Pilots from all nations waged war in single-seat fighter planes mounted with machine guns—one of the most notorious new weapons of the war.

Baron Manfred von Richthofen.

Early in the fighting, a new word entered the vocabulary of warfare: ace. Any pilot on either side was called an ace once he had downed five enemy aircraft. The French invented the term, but it was soon adopted by the other countries in the war and has remained with us to this day. At first, it was a major feat to knock five enemies out of the sky, but improvements in the guns soon made that number seem low. Germany did not crown a pilot an ace until he had had ten victories.

All the major fighting nations in Europe produced ace pilots. Germany's Baron Manfred von Richthofen surpassed all fliers in the number of victories. He downed eighty enemy planes before his death in April 1918, when he brought his scarlet-colored Fokker down to treetop level in pursuit of a British fighter and was struck by Australian ground fire.

Ranking right behind the Baron was the greatest of the British aces, Major Edward Mannock. Although he was blind in one eye, he scored seventy-three victories.

The United States was able to boast its share of aces, too. Their victories were far fewer than those recorded by the fliers of other nations because America had entered the war so late, but they were still impressive. Among the nation's leading aces were Lieutenant Frank Luke, Major Raoul Lufbery, and Captain Edward Rickenbacker.

FRANK LUKE

In September 1918, Frank Luke won fame for his attacks on German observation balloons. Carrying one to three men with sidearms, the balloons hovered aloft at the end of a cable and were used to direct artillery fire. Although they seemed to be helpless targets, they were defended by antiaircraft guns and swarms of fighter planes, so they were shunned by pilots.

The daring Luke found them inviting. On September 12, he dove in and turned one into a flaming mass. He shot down several more in the next days, only to have his luck run out on September 29. While downing his first balloon that day, a squadron of Fokkers blasted him with machine-gun fire, damaged his Spad, and seriously wounded him. Ignoring his pain, he attacked twice again and watched his targets explode into flames. He then ran for home, but was forced to land in an enemy-held field. German soldiers closed in and ordered him to surrender. He replied with his pistol. Seconds later, he lay dead from rifle fire. In that one month, he had downed fourteen balloons.

RAOUL LUFBERY

A leading ace with seventeen victories, Raoul Lufbery had one of the longest flying records in the war. He went to France in 1916 and joined the Lafayette Escadrille, a squadron manned by volunteer Americans and named for the Marquis de Lafayette, the young French officer who served under George Washington in the American Revolution.

When America joined the fighting, Lufbery transferred to the U.S. Army Air Service, was named commander of the 94th Aero Pursuit Squadron, and, in early 1918, led the first American flight over enemy lines. Tragically, his command of the 94th lasted only a short time.

On May 19, his plane caught fire during a dogfight. Without a parachute (they were not carried at the time), Raoul Lufbery threw himself clear of his burning cockpit and fell to his death. He was above a small river and may have been trying to save his life by plunging into the water.

EDWARD "EDDIE" RICKENBACKER

The honor of being America's top ace went to Eddie Rickenbacker. A well-known race-car driver before the war, he traveled overseas in his twenties as General Pershing's chauffeur. Soon he began to take flying lessons in his spare time. He became such an expert pilot that he was sent to Lufbery's 94th Aero Pursuit Squadron in March 1918.

Rickenbacker scored his first victory late that month and soon followed it with four more to win the title of ace. In September, he followed the downed Lufbery as

Ace pilot Eddie Rickenbacker, in front of his fighter plane, *France,* 1918.

the 94th's commander. He recorded another twenty-one victories before the war's end in November, giving him a total of twenty-six and making him America's foremost ace. He went on to a long career as an airline executive and died in 1973.

ON MANY FRONTS

The airplane did not serve only above France and Germany. It was also active in other combat areas: in Italy and Turkey, and above the Mediterranean and the Pacific. It also played a part in naval warfare.

Seaplanes were used for reconnaissance by both the British and U.S. navies. Both navies also outfitted their seaplanes with torpedoes and sent them out as bombers.

The British launched one of the first aircraft carriers, the *Ark Royal*. The ship was not like today's carriers. It did not launch its planes from its deck; rather, it carried seaplanes that were lowered by crane into the ocean for takeoff. Deck takeoffs began with the *Furious*, a British cruiser that was fitted with short runways fore and aft of its bridge. The first carrier strike in history was launched from the *Furious* in July 1918. Seven planes took off to bomb the German dirigible base at Tondern.

World War I proved that the airplane was a valuable weapon. It would show its full—and often terrible—value in wars later in the century.

WEAPONS OF WORLD WAR I

POISON GAS: The Germans, the first to use poison gas in the war, unleashed it on the Allied forces during the battles near Ypres in 1915. Soon thereafter, the Allies began producing gases of their own, and gas masks were added to the cumbersome equipment carried by soldiers on both sides.

One of the most widely used gases was mustard gas. It burned the victim's eyes, mouth, throat, and lungs, but did not often prove fatal. In 1925, attendees at an international convention at Geneva, Switzerland, agreed that gas was a savage

American soldiers of the 16th Infantry 1st Division in France, equipped with gas masks to protect themselves from the poison gases used in warfare.

weapon that could harm not only military personnel but civilian populations as well, and they banned its use in future wars.

THE TANK: Though employed by both sides at the time of World War I, the tank was a young and clumsy thing with the bad habit of breaking down. In 1916, in the first tank attack of the war, three dozen British tanks broke down while in an assault against the enemy. The tank's overall performance in the war, however, held the promise that it would one day be a frightening mobile weapon. That promise was fulfilled in World War II.

THE MACHINE GUN:This weapon dates from the 1700s, when the English produced a multibarreled gun that could be fired continuously by turning a hand crank. American inventor Richard Gatling improved the gun in the 1860s, producing a model operated by rapidly turning a series of barrels into firing position.

The machine gun attained its fame in World War I. In the trench warfare that dragged on from 1914 to early 1918, it was used to deadly effect in stopping enemy troops who were dashing across No Man's Land.

Men of the 80th Division in Meuse, France, firing a railway gun at a German position.

6

1918:
THE FATEFUL YEAR

THE ALLIED and Central Powers were in a dark mood as 1918 dawned. Each had suffered greatly in the major offensive of 1917—a giant Allied effort to smash through the German lines that extended for more than 150 miles (240 kilometers) from Ypres in Belgium to Reims in northeastern France.

The offensive, which raged from April to November, had won the Allies a few miles of enemy territory at the price of a terrible loss of life. In one battle near Reims, the French sustained 120,000 casualties in a mere five days. The final attacks in the Ypres area cost the British and Germans 240,000 casualties each and the French more than 8,500.

The Allied mood was further darkened by the news from other fronts. The Italians, drained by the fighting with Austria, were ready to abandon the war. In the east, the battered Russian people had revolted against their ruler, the czar, installed a new government in his place, and signed a peace treaty with Germany. The pact enabled Germany to shift its divisions there to the western front.

Despite this favorable turn of events for Germany, the mood there was as bleak as it was on the Allied side. The country was still being strangled by the British blockade. Austria-Hungary, Turkey, and Bulgaria were running out of resources and would soon be unable to continue fighting. To make matters worse, the newcomer, America, was shipping thousands of men to France.

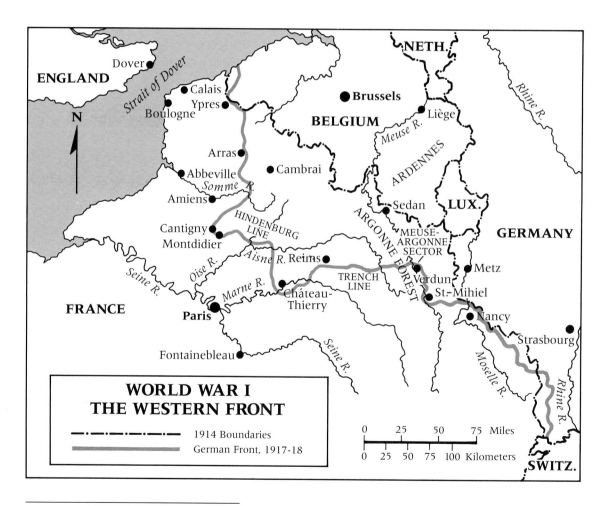

The arriving AEF troops were a major worry for General Erich von Ludendorff, co-commander (with General Paul von Hindenburg) of the German forces. He knew that as soon as they were on the scene in sufficient number, they could swing the war in the Allies' favor once and for all. Something now had to be done in 1918 to win a final victory.

THE LUDENDORFF OFFENSIVE

That "something" was a major offensive devised by the general. It was to be launched along the same front—from Ypres to Reims—that the Allies had attacked the year before. The front was shared by the British and the French. The British trenches extended more than halfway down from Ypres, and the French trenches continued the rest of the way to beyond Reims. Ludendorff planned to drive a wedge between the two by first hitting the British. Then he would push them over to the North Sea. There, with their backs against the water, he would hand them their final defeat, after which he would concentrate on destroying the French.

To accomplish the split, Ludendorff struck the British trenches that lay some 50 miles (80 kilometers) in front of the city of Amiens. The attack began on March 21 with a stunning five-hour bombardment by 6,000 cannons. Then sixty-two crack divisions stormed across No Man's Land and hurled the British back in confusion. In the next days, the German advanced 40 miles (64 kilometers) and began to close fast on Amiens. British reserves and regiments from the French lines rushed to the battle zone. Rallying the retreating frontline troops on April 5, they stalled Ludendorff short of Amiens.

German infantry in a trench raid against the British.

Four days later, the general loosed a second attack, this one far to the northwest. He sent his troops charging toward Ypres. After he took the city, the way would be clear for him to drive the enemy over to the North Sea. Because they were outnumbered, the British at first retreated, but on April 17 they regrouped and halted the advance, which had gained 10 miles (16 kilometers). They were not destined for a last stand with their backs against the water, as Ludendorff had planned.

Frustrated by the two failures, Ludendorff lashed out again. He hit the French lines near Reims. His moves against the British had failed in part because the French had come to their aid. Now he had two goals in mind: to bring the French dashing back to their own lines so that he could later hit the British with greater ease, and to begin the final defeat of France by closing in on Paris. The attack, launched on May 27, was aimed at the Marne River. Once across it, his army would be just 58 miles (93 kilometers) from the French capital.

During this attack on the Marne, the Americans began to play an important role in the war.

THE AMERICANS IN BATTLE

When Ludendorff began to move on the Marne, the AEF had nearly 400,000 men in its sector of trenches near the Swiss border, far distant from the front that was now under attack. General Pershing had earlier refused to let his men be absorbed into the Allied armies as replacements for lost soldiers. Now that the Germans were threatening Paris, Pershing offered to loan France's Marshal Ferdinand Foch, the supreme commander of the Allied forces, five divisions of the AEF for the Marne fighting. Foch gratefully accepted the offer.

Immediately, the units marched in to help the French. The 2nd and 3rd Divisions entrenched side by side on the Marne. The 3rd Division dug in at a place called Chateau Thierry and fended off an attack on May 30, helping to stall Ludendorff's move against the river.

The 2nd Division, manned by army and marine troops, took up a position 5 miles (8 kilometers) west of the 3rd Division, at the edge of Belleau Wood, a small forest that the Germans had recently captured. On June 6, the 2nd, with its marines in the lead, plunged into the woods. For five days, while being constantly raked by machine-gun fire, the Americans drove the Germans from the forest in hand-to-hand combat. Then the Americans and the French went on to clear a series of other enemy positions, bringing the latest phase in the Ludendorff offensive to a halt.

When compared to other battles, the actions at Chateau Thierry and Belleau Wood were small ones, but they proved to everyone on both sides that the Americans, despite their small amount of training, were formidable fighters.

The Americans also proved their worth elsewhere along the Marne. Among the troops that were loaned to Foch were four black units—the 369th, 370th, 371st, and 372nd Infantry Regiments. Though only on loan, they performed so well that Foch kept them as a part of the French army until war's end (though Pershing constantly asked for their return). These American soldiers wore French helmets and carried French arms.

The four regiments were National Guard units. Although they did not all come from the American South (the 369th, for example, was from New York State), the men were affectionately nicknamed "Dixie poilus" by their French comrades. *Poilu* is a French word for soldier.

The units, which were usually commanded by a combination of black and white officers, participated in a string of battles along the Marne, and several men won French decorations for courage in action. One soldier, Junius Diggs, a South Carolinian, braved enemy fire a half-dozen times to rescue and carry to safety friends who had stumbled on an enemy machine-gun nest. He was awarded France's highest military decoration, the Medaille Militaire.

In all, eight black National Guard regiments and two black regular army units served in the war. They were kept separate from white troops. The day when blacks and whites would serve together in the same unit would not come until after World War II.

THE ALLIES STRIKE BACK

Though he was meeting defeat everywhere, Ludendorff tried one more onslaught. In this attempt, aimed at Reims, he tried again to draw more French troops back to their lines and leave the British vulnerable to attack. Ludendorff triggered this latest and last action on the night of July 14–15. It was snuffed out within two days.

The general's offensive was finally over. It had raged for five months and had ended in disaster with the loss of more than 500,000 of his soldiers. The Allies had lost as many men, but were gaining rather than losing strength because Americans were continually arriving.

It was time for the Allies to retaliate.

The first blow was struck on August 8. In a surprise counterattack, a combined British-French force charged the German lines in front of Amiens and caught the enemy troops off guard. They panicked and fell back 10 miles (16 kilometers) in confusion. Regrouping, they tried to take up defensive positions—but to no avail. The swarming British and French units continued to uproot them and push them back to the line where the Ludendorff offensive had started in March. The German ranks were so tattered by September that Ludendorff ordered a further retreat of 15 miles (24 kilometers) to the Hindenburg Line. The Line, more than 40 miles (64 kilometers) long, bristled with concrete fortifications that the Germans had built as a final defense system in the event of an overwhelming Allied offensive. They believed it was too strong ever to be breached.

The Americans were the next to strike. After helping to stem the German tide on the Marne, they shifted to the St. Mihiel salient. The salient was a bulge that the Germans had made in the Allied lines southeast of Reims in 1914 and had held ever since. It was named for the town that stood just behind its forward point.

Pershing now had about a million men under his command, and the AEF had just been given a new name: the American First Army. The general was determined to wrest the salient from the Germans. He assigned ten divisions—a total of about 665,000 troops—to the task.

The St. Mihiel campaign began on the rainy morning of September 12. Before the American troops—or doughboys, as they were called, perhaps because of the hardtack biscuits they ate in the field—moved forward, Pershing hit the enemy with a 3,200-gun bombardment and the greatest air raid of the war.

Nearly 1,500 planes, including fighters and bombers, took part in the raid, all of them under the command of Colonel Billy Mitchell, the chief of the American Air Service. They knifed through the gray morning air to strafe trenches, set observation balloons afire (this was the day Frank Luke destroyed his first balloon), and bomb artillery positions. The aircraft were flown by British, French, Italian, Portuguese, and American pilots. The U.S. fliers numbered 609. The raid was a success, but not a spectacular one because the rain and mist made accurate bombing difficult.

The spectacular success came when the doughboys

The 18th Infantry, Machine Gun Battalion, en route to the St. Mihiel Front.

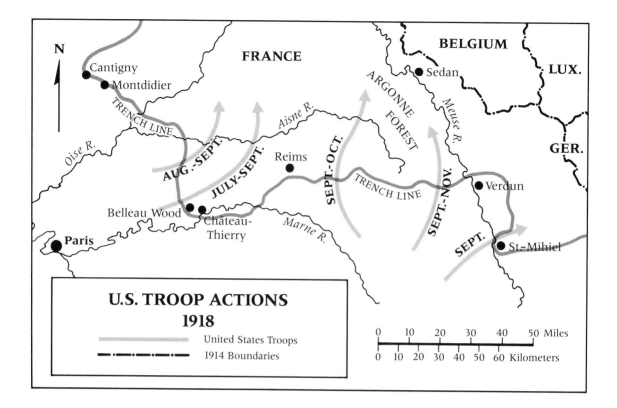

and a fleet of U.S. tanks surged into the battle. Fighting in sticky mud, they advanced so quickly that the town of St. Mihiel was in their hands within 48 hours. With the Germans surrendering at some points and fighting fiercely at others, the Americans cleared the salient by September 16. In four days of fighting, 16,000 prisoners and 450 artillery pieces had fallen into U.S. hands.

The victory was a major one for the doughboys, who were fast becoming battle-hardened veterans. The next feat was even greater: the taking of the Meuse-Argonne sector.

THE FINAL PUSH

At the beginning of 1918, Marshall Foch believed that, with the Americans now lending a hand, Germany would collapse in 1919 and the war would end. The great success of the British-French counterattack from Amiens, however, convinced him that the Allies did not need to wait that long. The Germans were bleeding and staggering. A massive Allied offense could deliver a blow that would be fatal in a matter of weeks.

Foch decided to strike with an all-out offensive from the North Sea to the city of Verdun, approximately 60 miles (96 kilometers) beyond Reims. The U.S. role in the offensive would be to clear the Meuse-Argonne sector near Reims.

American tanks and General John J. Pershing's doughboys advanced into battle to take the St. Mihiel salient.

Troops, trucks, horses, and tanks in the muddy trek to Argonne.

Pershing was told of his new assignment as he was planning the St. Mihiel attack. The general could have canceled his St. Mihiel plans, but he decided that his men could handle both tasks. Consequently, when the St. Mihiel fighting ended on September 16, he had to move his giant army 50 miles (80 kilometers) to the Meuse-Argonne. The new offensive was to begin on September 26, which gave him less than two weeks to get there.

The responsibility for supervising the move went to his chief staff officer, Colonel George C. Marshall, who watched those two weeks turn into a horror. The troops had to march blindly at night so that the enemy would not be aware of what they were doing. With a constant mist dripping from their helmets, they slogged through thick mud, slept wherever they could when daylight came, and then cursed as they made their way again. Time and again, tanks, artillery, cars, and horse-drawn supply wagons became mired in the mud and lurched to a stop, creating a massive traffic jam. The thousands of French soldiers who choked the roads as they came down from the Meuse-Argonne to make room for the Americans made matters worse.

When the doughboys reached their destination, they found themselves on a front 24 miles (39 kilometers) wide. Studded with hills, valleys, and densely wooded lands, it stretched from the Meuse River on their right to the Argonne Forest on their left. With the heavy fortifications—networks of trenches, machine-gun nests, and artillery emplacements—that the Germans had built since occupying the area in 1914, it was brutal country to cross. The fortifications not only ranged across the width of the sector but extended back into it for 12 miles (19 kilometers).

Miraculously, the Americans—nine divisions on the front line and four to the rear in reserve—were in place when the offensive began on September 26. They met light resistance at first and advanced 3 miles (5 kilometers) on their first day.

Enemy resistance soon stiffened, however, and the fight for the Meuse-Argonne turned into a greater horror than the march to get there had been. The doughboys were caught in murderous crossfire whenever they advanced through a valley. Their units became separated in the maze of trees and trenches. They had to move forward by darting from tree to tree, firing at an unseen enemy. They fought an unending series of small battles as they routed enemy soldiers from trenches with bayonets or crawled up to machine-gun nests and silenced them with hand grenades or rifle fire.

At one point in the fighting, a battalion of more than 500 men forded a river at dusk and dug in for the night. By morning, they were surrounded by a German regiment. They refused to surrender because Pershing had issued orders to everyone that once any ground was taken it must never be abandoned. So these men endured artillery barrages and attacks for five days until friendly troops broke through. The unit won fame back home as the "Lost Battalion."

Some days later, seventeen men from the 82nd Division, working behind the enemy lines, crept up on a machine-gun nest and captured its crew. As they were preparing to take their prisoners to the rear, a German voice rang out from a nearby nest and ordered the crewmen to drop to the ground. The order was instantly obeyed. A split-second later, rattling gunfire ripped into the Americans, wounding three and killing six.

During the fierce fight with the Germans for the Meuse-Argonne, the American wounded found shelter in a shattered church in Neuilly, close to the Argonne Forest.

Sergeant Alvin C. York, of Pall Mall, Tennessee, on the hill where he captured 132 German prisoners on October 8, 1918.

Among the survivors was Alvin York, a young corporal from Tennessee. With his sergeant lying dead, he took command of the group, left his fellow survivors in charge of the prisoners, and began to crawl toward the nearby nest. He took shelter behind the trees as he moved, and then, being an excellent marksman, shot any German who poked his head above the sandbag surrounding the nest.

So deadly was York's fire that the commander of the surrounding machine-gun positions shouted an offer to surrender his ninety men. The corporal lined the German crews up as they came to him with their arms upraised. Pressing the muzzle of his rifle into the back of the commander, York began to march back to the American lines. At the sight of the procession, the crews of other enemy machine-gun nests along the way also surrendered.

By the time he reached safety, Corporal York had taken an amazing number of prisoners: 132 in all. He was promoted to sergeant and was awarded the Congressional Medal of Honor.

Throughout October, the Americans fought their way forward. In the first days of November, they broke out of the Meuse-Argonne. Now Pershing's demand that all U.S. soldiers be trained in mobile warfare paid great dividends. The troops, once in open country, raced forward and by November 6 were threatening the city of Sedan.

While Pershing's troops had been working their way from tree to tree, other battles had raged along the German front. The British had broken through the Hindenburg Line on October 17. At the northwestern end of the front, British and Belgian troops began pushing the Germans back into Belgium and toward Germany.

All along the entire length of the front, the German army was cracking. The soldiers did not know it, but peace was just days away.

THE ELEVENTH HOUR, THE ELEVENTH DAY, THE ELEVENTH MONTH

WHILE THE BATTLES were raging on the western front, Germany's partners in the war—Austria-Hungary, Bulgaria, and Turkey—were being soundly beaten elsewhere. The situation was so desperate that at the close of September, Kaiser Wilhelm ordered a telegram to be sent to President Woodrow Wilson:

> To avoid further bloodshed, the German government requests the President to arrange the immediate conclusion of an armistice on land, by sea, and in the air.

The message pleased Wilson deeply. It also disturbed him because it ignored a matter that he considered of utmost importance. The telegram made no mention of whether the armistice would be based on what were known worldwide as his "Fourteen Points" for peace.

He had outlined these points in a speech before Congress in January 1918. He said that they should serve as the basis of any peace agreement with Germany. Only with them could the world become "a fit place to live in." They covered matters ranging from the freeing of Belgium to one that was close to his heart: the establishment of a world organization to settle future international disputes peacefully.

In his reply to Germany's message, Wilson asked if the armistice would be based on the Fourteen Points. Before Germany could answer, however, U-boats sank two passenger liners. The Allied world was enraged. Wilson told Germany that the Allies would not negotiate a peace but instead would be demanding an unconditional surrender. Backing the president's statement were David Lloyd George, prime minister of England, and Georges Clemenceau, premier of France.

By now, Germany's situation was more than desperate. Bulgaria surrendered in late September. Turkey followed suit on October 30. On November 3, British troops broke through the enemy lines in Belgium and began to attack the Germans from the rear. The next day, Austria-Hungary surrendered, after having been driven out of Italy by an Allied force.

The German people, starving and exhausted, were demanding peace. So were 100,000 of the nation's sailors. On November 4 they mutinied and seized control of the naval installations at Kiel and other ports. On the heels of the mutiny came an army revolt that ended when the troops established socialist governments in six cities, including Berlin, the nation's capital.

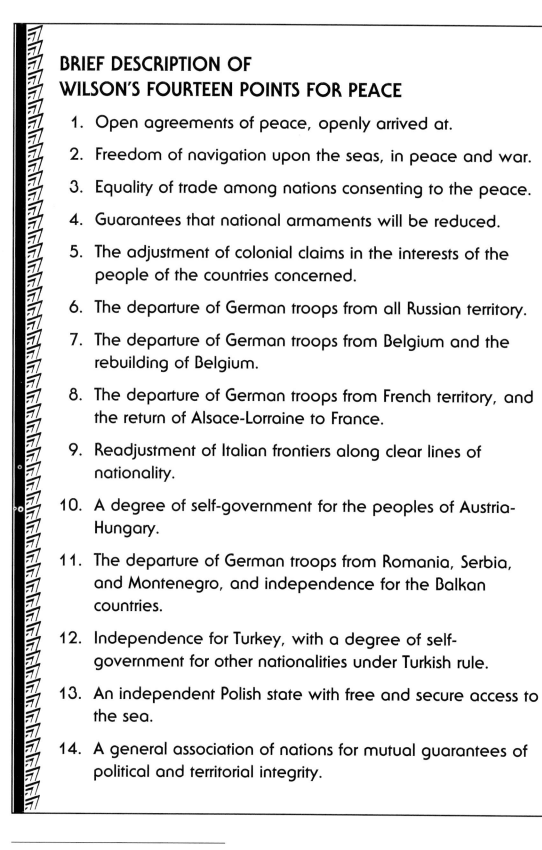

BRIEF DESCRIPTION OF
WILSON'S FOURTEEN POINTS FOR PEACE

1. Open agreements of peace, openly arrived at.

2. Freedom of navigation upon the seas, in peace and war.

3. Equality of trade among nations consenting to the peace.

4. Guarantees that national armaments will be reduced.

5. The adjustment of colonial claims in the interests of the people of the countries concerned.

6. The departure of German troops from all Russian territory.

7. The departure of German troops from Belgium and the rebuilding of Belgium.

8. The departure of German troops from French territory, and the return of Alsace-Lorraine to France.

9. Readjustment of Italian frontiers along clear lines of nationality.

10. A degree of self-government for the peoples of Austria-Hungary.

11. The departure of German troops from Romania, Serbia, and Montenegro, and independence for the Balkan countries.

12. Independence for Turkey, with a degree of self-government for other nationalities under Turkish rule.

13. An independent Polish state with free and secure access to the sea.

14. A general association of nations for mutual guarantees of political and territorial integrity.

Ferdinand Foch.

Ludendorff, broken by his failures on the western front, resigned his post on October 26, leaving his co-commander, General Paul von Hindenburg, in charge of the disintegrating army.

The growing revolt inside Germany led to the country's establishment of a socialist government on November 9. The next day, Kaiser Wilhelm fled Berlin and settled in the Netherlands, where he remained until his death in 1941.

While Kaiser Wilhelm was fleeing, a German delegation met with Marshal Foch in a railway car in the Forest of Compiègne. Throughout the night, the delegation heard Foch describe the Allied terms for an armistice. He told them that Germany must immediately vacate all the territory it had taken in the fighting; hand over all its submarines and place its surface warships in ports specified by the Allies; surrender all its war materials; and return all Allied prisoners.

The delegation agreed to the terms at dawn on November 11, 1918, and the armistice took effect at 11:00 A.M. that same day. Weary soldiers on both sides put down their arms. A welcome quiet spread over the world.

At the eleventh hour of the eleventh day of the eleventh month of 1918, the fighting ended.

THE TREATY OF VERSAILLES

The armistice ended the fighting, but the treaty that marked the formal close of the war was signed in 1919, when representatives from the Allied states met in France for the Paris Peace Conference. Among them were the "Big Four"—Britain's Prime Minister David Lloyd George, France's Premier Georges Clemenceau, Italy's Premier Vittorio Orlando, and America's President Woodrow Wilson.

German representatives watched as the Treaty of Versailles was drawn up; they were allowed no voice in the Conference.

The treaty set out a variety of terms on which the peace was to be based:

> The complete disarmament of Germany, with the Allies agreeing to reduce their own armaments.
>
> The payment of reparations by Germany to make up for the financial losses sustained by the Allies during the war. The amount to be paid was to be decided later by a special commission.

The "Big Four" (from left to right): Britain's Prime Minister David Lloyd George, Italy's Premier Vittorio Orlando, France's Premier Georges Clemenceau, and U.S. President Woodrow Wilson.

The adjustment of certain European borders in favor of the Allied nations (such as the establishment of Czechoslovakia as an independent state and the return to France of Alsace-Lorraine, which it had lost to Germany in the Franco-Prussian war of 1870).

The transfer of all German colonies to the Allies.

The removal of all German troops from Serbia, the little nation whose terrorists had been responsible for igniting the war by plotting the assassination of Austria's Archduke Ferdinand.

Immediately after the armistice of 1918, Serbia and five of its neighboring countries joined hands to form the nation of Yugoslavia. Bosnia, where Ferdinand had met his death, and its neighbor Hercegovina entered the nation as a single member state. The other member states were Croatia, Macedonia, Slovenia, and Montenegro.

In World War II, communist factions took over Yugoslavia and dominated it until the late 1980s. Since then, the nation, which had always been the scene of trouble among its various ethnic groups, has been torn asunder by civil strife.

The pact both disappointed and heartened Wilson. It disappointed him because it took into account only a few of his Fourteen Points, such as the promise by the Allies to reduce the number of their armaments (a promise that was only partially kept). He took heart, however, from the fact that it included a provision to establish the organization that he and other peace-loving leaders had long hoped for. That organization was the League of Nations, a body of countries that would seek to avoid war by working to settle international disputes peaceably.

While in Paris, Wilson worked tirelessly to have the idea for the League of Nations included in the Treaty of

Versailles. These efforts ended in success, and the treaty required all the nations that signed it to become members of the League. But the president's efforts at home on behalf of the organization ended in disappointment for him and ruined his health. The U.S. Congress, loath to become again entangled in foreign disputes, was vehemently opposed to having the United States join the League. In an effort to get the public to force a change of the congressional mind, Wilson undertook a nationwide speaking tour. Wherever he went, he argued in favor of the League and called it essential for lasting world peace.

Exhausted by his work in Paris and by the speaking tour, the president suffered a stroke on September 25, 1919, after making a speech in Pueblo, Colorado. Though the stroke left him partially paralyzed for the rest of his life, it did not stop him from speaking out for the League from his bed.

But his efforts went for naught. In 1919 the Senate rejected the treaty because of its requirement that any signing nation must become a member of the League. The United States then went on to make a separate peace agreement with Germany in 1921.

As wise as the idea was, the League of Nations turned out to be a disappointment in the long run. It was powerless to stop the aggressions that led to World War II, although it paved the way for today's United Nations. Though it would have nothing to do with the League, the United States became a prime mover in the establishment of the United Nations, which replaced the League in 1945.

The Treaty of Versailles, despite the U.S. refusal to sign the pact, formally ended the greatest war that the world had ever seen. Altogether, it had cost the warring

Parade in New York City, 1919, welcoming American soldiers home from the war. More than 50,000 Americans had been killed in "the war to end all wars" and more than 200,000 wounded.

nations more than $281 billion. Worse was its cost in human lives.

More than 65 million men took part in the fighting—some 42 million for the Allies and more than 22.5 million for the Central Powers. Almost 4.9 million Allied soldiers lost their lives and 12.8 million were wounded. Losses for the Central Powers numbered more than 3 million dead and 8.4 million wounded. America had contributed 4.3 million men and had suffered the deaths of more than 50,000. More than 205,000 had been wounded.

World War I was a conflict that Wilson called "the war to end all wars." He was mistaken. Tragically, it proved to be the first conflict in a century that would be scarred by warfare throughout its entire course.

MAJOR FIGURES IN A FUTURE WAR

These men who served in World War I also became major figures in World War II:

HARRY S. TRUMAN (1884–1972)

The thirty-third president of the United States served as a captain with the 129th Field Artillery in France. He was elected to the U.S. Senate in 1934, headed a Senate committee investigating American military spending during World War II, became vice president in 1944, and entered the White House in 1945 on the death of Franklin D. Roosevelt.

ADOLF HITLER (1889–1945)

The German dictator who triggered World War II joined the army in 1914 and served until 1918, rising to the rank of corporal. He was twice wounded and earned the Iron Cross, 1st Class.

DOUGLAS MACARTHUR (1880–1964)

A colonel (later a brigadier general) with the 42nd Division during the war, MacArthur went on to become army chief of staff in 1930. He twice held army commands in the Philippines and, on his retirement in 1937, served as an adviser to the Philippine army. At the outbreak of World War II, he was recalled to U.S. Army service and was named supreme allied commander in Southeast Asia.

GEORGE S. PATTON (1885–1945)

A colonel, a tank commander, and a close friend of Douglas MacArthur in World War I, Patton rose to the rank of general and commanded the U.S. Third Army in World War II, establishing himself as one of the finest battlefield officers in U.S. history.

DWIGHT D. EISENHOWER (1890–1969)

A lieutenant at the time America entered the war, Eisenhower did not go overseas but was assigned to several training camps at home. He worked as MacArthur's administrative assistant in the

1930s. In World War II, Eisenhower was named supreme commander of the Western Allied Forces. Following the war, he served as military commander of the North Atlantic Treaty Organization. Eisenhower was elected the nation's thirty-fourth president in 1952.

HERMANN GOERING (1893–1946)
On Baron von Richthofen's death, Goering was named commander of Richthofen's flying unit. In the 1920s, he aligned himself with Hitler, rose high in the Nazi party, and commanded the German Air Force in World War II. With other Nazi leaders, he was tried for war crimes in 1945–1946, was found guilty, and was sentenced to death. He cheated the hangman by committing suicide.

ERWIN ROMMEL (1891–1944)
An infantry lieutenant in 1914, Rommel later became Germany's foremost authority on tank warfare. He was nicknamed "The Desert Fox" for his brilliant North African campaigns in World War II. Named a field marshal, he took command of western Europe's defense when the Allied invasion of 1944 loomed. Later, Rommel was accused of participating in the German plot to assassinate Hitler, but was not prosecuted. Instead Hitler's representatives gave him the choice of committing suicide or having his death reported as the result of wounds. He chose to take his own life.

GEORGE C. MARSHALL (1880–1959)
Marshall served as a staff officer under Pershing. In World War II, with the rank of general, he directed U.S. operations in both Europe and the Pacific. He was appointed U.S. secretary of state by President Truman in 1947 and, while in that post, inaugurated the Marshall Plan to facilitate the economic recovery of Europe in the wake of the war. In 1953 the general was awarded the Nobel Peace Prize for the plan.

BIBLIOGRAPHY

Asprey, Robert B. *At Belleau Wood.* New York: G.P. Putnam's Sons, 1965.

Aviation Classics from Aviation Quarterly. Dallas: *Aviation Quarterly,* 1984.

Bruce, Anthony. *An Illustrated Companion to the First World War.* London: Michael Joseph, 1989.

Coffman, Edward M. *The War to End All Wars.* New York: Oxford University Press, 1968.

Fraser, David. *Knight's Cross: A Life of Field Marshal Erwin Rommel.* New York: HarperCollins, 1993.

Funderburk, Thomas R. *The Early Birds of War: The Daring Pilots and Fighter Aeroplanes of World War I.* New York: Grosset & Dunlap, 1968.

Gray, Edwyn A. *The U-Boat War: 1914–1918.* London: Leo Cooper, 1994.

Grenville, J.A.S. *A History of the World in the Twentieth Century.* Cambridge, Mass.: Harvard University Press, 1994.

Harbord, James G. *The American Army in France, 1917–1919.* Boston: Little, Brown, 1936.

Kennedy, David M. *Over Here: The First World War and American Society.* New York: Oxford University Press, 1980.

Kennet, Lee. *The First Air War: 1914–1918.* New York: Macmillan, 1991.

Lawson, Don. *The United States in World War I.* New York: Scholastic Book Services, 1964.

Morison, Samuel Eliot. *The Oxford History of the American People: 1869 to the Death of John F. Kennedy 1963.* Volume 3. New York: Oxford University Press, 1965.

Palmer, Frederick. *America in France.* New York: Dodd, Mead, 1918.

Peterson, C., and Gilbert C. Fite. *Opponents of War, 1917–1918.* Seattle: University of Washington Press, 1957.

Roberts, J.M. *History of the World.* New York: Oxford University Press, 1993.

Schneider, Dorothy, and Carl J. Schneider. *Into the Breach: American Women Overseas in World War I.* New York: Viking Penguin, 1991.

Shermer, David. *World War I.* London: Octopus Books, 1973.

Stallings, Laurence. *The Doughboys: The Story of the AEF, 1917–1918.* New York: Harper & Row, 1963.

Toland, John. *No Man's Land: 1918—The Last Year of the Great War.* New York: Konecky and Konecky, 1980.

Tuchman, Barbara W. *The Guns of August.* New York: Macmillan, 1962.

INDEX